S0-BNH-218

HANDIWORK

To Michael McFee,

With admiration and
every good wish—

Jim Clark

Christmas 1998

Also by Jim Clark:

Dancing On Canaan's Ruins

HANDIWORK

poems by

Jim Clark

St. Andrews College Press
Laurinburg, North Carolina
1998

This book is made possible through the
Richard Walser & Bernice Kelley Harris Fund
of the St. Andrews College Press

Copyright © 1998 by Jim Clark

Library of Congress Cataloging-in-Publication Data

Clark, Jim 1954. Handiwork / Jim Clark—
Laurinburg, NC / St. Andrews College Press
I. Clark, Jim. II. Title

St. Andrews College Press
1700 Dogwood Mile
Laurinburg, NC 28352

ISBN: 1-879934-59-0

Cover design: Dan Auman
Cover photo of Vollis Simpson's windmills: Jim Clark
Author photo: Keith Tew

Typeset in Old Claude

First Printing: November 1998

In memory of my maternal grandmother

Agnes Donaldson Terry
(1896-1987)

the voice of all my stories

Contents

EN PASSANT

Handiwork	2
Once More, the Night	4
Letter to Ciardi: April 3, 1986	6
Hearing Creeley Read	8
Fortune's Favorite Child	9
Aging Gracefully	10
No Love Lost	12
En Passant: At Dinner	14
You	16

LANDSCAPES, VOICES

A Short History of Place	18
Three Voices from Hunter's Point	19
Sunday Dinner	20
The Land Under the Lake	22
Miss Ida Belle McHenry Talks to the Man from the State "Stories from Our Seniors" Project	23
Moonrise at Dale Hollow Lake	27
House Burning	28
Reeling In	33

The Reverend Moody Montgomery Takes
    Up Serpents for the First and Last Time   35
Working for Roger   48
John Lee Hooker   57

LEARNING HOW TO LIVE

Loveless You Wander   60
In Thrall   62
Winding Down   63
After Rilke   64
Last Summer When the Moon   67
The Life You've Led   68
How It Was   69
Night Music   70
Lights   71
Climbing   72
The Naked Man in Briars   73
Ballade: Les Enfants du Soleil   74
Learning How to Live   76

Acknowledgments   77
Notes   78
About the Author   79

EN PASSANT

Handiwork

—for Jane Taylor

The figure of the woman in the garden,
the brightly colored fruit poised at her lips,
is not archetypal—she is a friend of mine.
Granted, she has known some good, some evil,
but she has come by such knowledge honestly.

She has met me here to help
build a barn. All morning
we have been raising beams, supports,
until now, near noon, we lie
in the long grass looking
at the wood skeleton, all done
but for a couple of ribs.

We drowse for a spell
and after awhile begin again.
It's hard work—sweat
sheets our foreheads, arms.
We move surely, methodically, knowing
what comes next. Across the river
our echoing hammers build nothing.
Hours pass.

Suddenly, from deep in the canebrake,
something thrashes, cries,
struggles into the air,

then falls, breaking
into our rhythm of work.

It is a young quail, not able
to fly. My friend puts down her hammer
and gathers the bird into her hands.
Quietly, evening rises about us,
breathing out from plants,
from soil and water.
Now and again the quail peeps.
From the slick leaf mold at our feet
a cricket rasps
its dark counterpoint.

Once More, the Night

Black rock under no moon,
stars, Jupiter cradled
in the dip of the southern ridge
where the power lines scissor up
toward the horizon's faint borealis.

Below, on the black mirror of the lake,
a small fishing boat purrs
into Bonner's Cove. Ripples shatter
the starlit water. A single match
flares, goes out, the orange coal
of a cigarette brightening.

"I'm getting married," you say,
cracking another beer.
I shift my weight against a rock
and smile. I know her, the quiet
dark-skinned woman with the strong hands.
I look down at the boat, drifting
in the cove. Years from now,
it will be you down there,
and your wife and children, baiting
the hooks by a hissing yellow lantern,
setting the jugs afloat, the children
shrieking with delight at the huge
channel cat floundering in the boat.

The cooler between us empties.
I don't tell you I've decided
to go west, soon. You get up
to take a piss and startle
an owl in the cedars behind us.
"*Otus asio,*" you say,
"The common screech owl, bane
of faint-hearted campers everywhere."
Laughing, you walk unsteadily
toward the woods. Your white shirt
ripples in the breeze, outlined
against the dark. From where I lie
you could be a spirit, moving
intently through a familiar wood—
William Bartram come ghostly downriver,
notebook in hand, eyes
full of bluebell and trillium,
a tale of the fierce alligator gar
on your tongue.

        When you come back
there's already a glow in the east,
and the fishing boat's making for
Redmond's Landing. You hand me a beer
and we finish the last two.

Letter to Ciardi: April 3, 1986

Dear Mr. Ciardi:

I have before me yours of March 28
in which you say "It's much in my mind
that I expected to be on my way
to Denver today." Well, that's the way
of travel—always that uncertainty, always
an element of danger. I much appreciate
your regrets, which you say are real and deep.
You were of course missed, but the festival
went off without a hitch—better, even,
than we dared hope.

I am sorry to hear of your illness—
as for death being the easy way out, I suppose
I haven't lived long enough
to offer an opinion. You say you are sorry
you have failed us—you have not.
As I said, we had great success,
beautiful weather, and everyone
seemed happy, even jubilant.
You say you have taken some massive injections
and feel you may become human again
in a few more days. Good.
No simple project, that.
The flesh is weak but sometimes must guide
the spirit in its blindness.

And speaking of blindness, as I write
snow from a spring storm blows and swirls
outside my office window. The jonquils
have slipped under, leaving no trace.
How fickle the weather is in Denver!

I thank you for your kind
letter of apology. Rest assured
all is well, and do not concern yourself
overmuch with our affairs.

I must close. Already the power is out
in several areas. The road home
is treacherous and difficult to negotiate
and the hoary limbs of great trees
are falling everywhere.

Hearing Creeley Read

Trees whisper—
winter stalks
dry leaves.

Birds' shadows
pour down dark
ghost-tongued
fire.

New signs
burn
ice-bright in this
wood.

Fortune's Favorite Child

Anderson is mad, this everyone knows.
In his skiff, his crafty house, Anderson rows

Out to the island. Gray sky, gray water—
Fortune's favorite child, driven to loiter.

Bones of fish in the sky, stars in the sea—
Anderson on the beach, musing intently:

"No man is an island," the poet said,
And Anderson agrees, though sometimes in his head

The ocean's mystic current swirls and swells
Around the core of him so that Anderson dwells

A man apart, obscure, a mystery more
Mist enshrouded than the beach, this morning at four.

He shakes off the spell, turns the skiff on its side,
Settling down to work at the edge of the tide.

Driftwrack and seaspawn and among them moving
Like old men in a strange land the crabs, loving

The littoral world of stink and rot.
Anderson paints them red and blue; a spot

Of morning coffee on the napkin darkens a claw.
Anderson paints on, incorporates the flaw.

Aging Gracefully

We are men, in our late thirties,
and we have set the neighbor's roof afire.
"Flaming Balls," the packages read,
crude lettering provocatively purpling
the flimsy cardboard, shrink-wrapped and
innocently lying in their silver-dusty bin
at Big Ed's State Line Fireworks Supermarket,
Chattanooga, TN. The inscrutable logo
should have warned but didn't: A lone rocket
atop a pair of cherry bombs.

Now, in this sultry suburb of the city
Sherman burned, the last gleam of twilight
fading in the west, to the fevered delight
of our attendant offspring we have
lit the fuse, and we have run away.

Independence flowers overhead, reflected
in our wistful eyes. Seconds later,
a woman's voice calls from the porch, "I see
something over there. A light. *There.*"
We turn as one, and there— *There!*—
the loose shag of dry pine needles littering
the neighbor's roof erupts in fiery cascade.

In the acrid dark we clamber over chain-link
as tall as a man—slip, rip, howl and we are in.

Someone is pulling a bucking, sputtering hose
through a chain-link diamond, and in my stomach
beer loses ground to flaming Hot Wings, the inner
world mirroring the outer. Through mist and smoke
and lurid flame dimly I see three figures
on the roof, stomping out flames, sweating,
bent double. Some herky-jerky Outback ritual
dance unfolds, complete with rhythmic chant—
Anybody home? Oh, Anybody home!—and I think
I must be dreaming.

                         Stillness. Startled silence.
Then bodies, damp and smudged, slide from the roof.
Show's over. Nobody's home. Wind in the empty garden
hose moans like a didgeridoo.

The fire truck slunk back to the station.
The Sheriff let us off with a warning.
The neighbors came home drunk and didn't notice.
The women put the children to bed and talked
low on the porch, long into the night. We knew
to stay away. Sometime later on a breath of wind
came the chuckled whisper— *"Flaming Balls!"*

No Love Lost

—for J.D.

Caroline, the world warms to whiskey.
In an artful striptease it slides
from its veils
stands forth shivering
and burns.
I burn, and shivering
clasp you to me.
Old friend, we survived
even love.

I see you now with an eye
whetted by distance and time—
Jed gone, and you a widow at twenty-nine.
No love lost now between us
in this house of old friends
where the music swells and sweeps us
into the sinuous world of the waltz.
We glide easily among other bodies,
subject to the laws of our own dear universe:
Gravity: the attraction of bodies, this dance.
Entropy: the losses—
Bill by accident.
Maggie, confusion.
Jed by whiskey and his own hand.

Good God! "No love lost between us,"
I said. He's gone, who was both
husband and friend. He'd love
the irony. I can almost hear him
weirdly intoning: *Who is the third
who walks always beside you?*

Enough. What else to say? We loved
him too well, too long—
could not see beyond the dazzling mask
he wore those late nights edging
into exhausted morning. *The freshness of night
has been fresh a long time,* he'd say
to the moon or to me as we stumbled
home along the abandoned railroad tracks.

Caroline, hold me. You take the lead.
This waltzing cuts bone-close,
weaving, as we do, among friends,
among ghosts.

En Passant: At Dinner

I would, if I could, say, "You must excuse me, I
foreign to this place. Your language is strange to
the things that you do." And then just shut up. I
no one would question me, and I could go on al
eating unnoticed. They would come to think of me
as some sort of fixture—a wooden Indian, perhap
but gathering dust, half hid in a corner. But I cann
My accent would give me away.

So I sit at this table and look out at all the people,
like the fingers of a balled-up fist. I will not be al
here like this for long—unnoticed, watching. Alr
fist is unclenching, the fingers stretching towards

The waitress comes and deposits my clams on th
She is pleasant, says little, speaks softly. But I do n
her. I am looking down, scowling, thinking of so
else. I am thinking: *I wish I could tunnel my wa*
this scowl my face is frozen into. I part my lips, b
eyes, wiggle my ears. But it is too much effort. I'r
in here. I remember I wanted it this way.

Conversations whir about in the air around me lik
night beetles, only half aware of their wings—crashing into
the screens of ears, burning up in the lamps of mouths. I
smile slightly, somewhere inside. But I do not smile for long,

because I know all the things of which they speak. Even the collisions and enjambments are familiar. I cannot deny it.

Still looking down, I murmur to myself: "These voices crept by me upon the waters ..." "Excuse me?" It is the waitress, come again. She is puzzled. I think: *'Excuse me.' Structure: apology. No. Wrong inflection. Not an apology.* Then suddenly I am back: the dim restaurant smelling of fish and vinegar, the buzz of conversations, the waitress, expectant. I think to myself: *It should be perfectly obvious, dear lady— I am talking to my clams.* But I do not say this. Instead, I look up at her great wondrous eyes, and I say "Nothing." Because that is what I mean. She leaves, uncertainly, and I am alone with my clams.

A thought suggests itself violently: *No—Wrong—The faces, the people—it is not a fist at all, but an octopus uncoiling. And this tentacle snaking my way is a red-faced man with a cigar.* But perhaps there is still time. If I can just ... "Excuse me," says the red-faced man. It is too late. I am found out. I know the language and must speak.

You

You are the pronoun of my dreams.
You are what listens
when, in all honesty confessing
my powerlessness in this world,
all I can do is call, and you
are what I call.

You are the foil of language,
sigil of the contrary,
anathema of echo. You are
the waiting lifeboat
disappearing into fog.

You are the only thing between.

You are what waits
in delirious anticipation
for my tongue to enter
and always I press
toward the mark
of your high calling.

In spite of my teachers
you are the stubborn one
whose nerves are the abacus wires
upon which move the beads
of my particular pain, each word
a calculus of desire.

In this desert, this aridity
of self, you are the spider
that sorts and strings the pearls of dew.

LANDSCAPES, VOICES

A Short History of Place

Difficult

Defeated

Nameless

Only

Three Voices from Hunter's Point

1

I's a Christian
fer 'bout three months
a year'r so ago—
Danged if I don't wish
I hadn jist
gone ahead'n died then.

2

Well, reckon I'm a-gittin' old—
I'd shore give a purty penny
to be eighteen agin,
but Lord God
ye jist don't git sec'nts
down that road.

3

Thank you kindly boys,
but y'all can jist let me out here—
I'd sooner be two hours late
as lay a corpse thirty minutes.

Sunday Dinner

"Go and bring a hen to the smokehouse door,"
My grandmother said when I was eight years old.
Dust motes swam in sunlit shafts, as four
Birds roosting eyed me, venomous and bold.

The one on the right, a fat, querulous thing,
Cocked her sequined eye as under her I slid
A trembling hand. I blinked, she struck, my ring
Finger oozed red, jumped in my pocket and hid.

"Now go and get Betty," my grandmother said.
"Tell her to bring water, a knife and some salt."
I looked and I looked, but Betty had fled;
I ran to the smokehouse and ground to a halt.

A shower of red rained down on my head;
My hurt finger quickened, and my heart raced.
My grandmother's apron from her lap bled
Scarlet drops onto her dusty shoes unlaced,

As round my legs a small white fury danced,
A feathery balloon someone let go.
At its head, or where its head should be, I glanced,
Recoiling in terror at its dumb show.

And that was Saturday noon. Sabbath morn,
We arose and to the meetinghouse went.
And when the preacher said "Ye must be reborn—"
"Washed in the blood—" I knew what he meant.

When the song of invitation sprang
From lips in dark faces I thought I knew,
I made my way down the aisle as they sang
And faced the preacher, and tried to answer true.

I stood in water, the back of my head
Cupped in his right hand. I answered again
The questions he posed, and afterwards fed
On the grape and the bread, though my mind in circles ran.

So home we went, and, famished, awaited word
Of blessing—the Sunday table, steaming, spread
With the bounty of earth, the crisp, golden bird.
We ate the blood and the body. We resurrected the dead.

The Land Under the Lake

*—for my parents, on the occasion
of their 50th Wedding Anniversary*

I think of Noah, his family spared,
Riding that bark of gopher wood above
The good lands of home, now submarine, paired
Beasts below waiting for news of the dove.

Less sublime than God's wondrous instruction,
The voice of the Washington bureaucrat
Told of the Dale Hollow Dam's construction—
Good farms, long held, flooded in nothing flat.

One summer on a houseboat we drifted
Over barns and churches, cornfields and cribs,
Swam down, down, to where gauzy light sifted
Like silt through some barn's or house's ribs.

Marriage is an ark, with children safe below,
And love is the land lying under the lake.
In the little drowned chapel years ago
My mother and father slice their wedding cake.

Miss Ida Belle McHenry Talks to the Man from the State "Stories from Our Seniors" Project

There was a woman lived over the ridge there,
Ruby Donaldson was her name, granddaughter
Of Rachel Donaldson, Andrew Jackson's wife.
The old Donaldson place is under the lake
Now, just out from the dam, about where
The swinging bridge crosses over from
Hickory Grove to the island. She had
An old open-back banjo that Clyde Forrest
Had made for her daddy, but he never learned
To play it. Miss Ruby picked it up
And got right good at it. She'd sit on her porch
In the evening in the hickory rocker,
With her back straight as a board, and she'd hold
That banjo with the neck straight up and down
And play "Soldier's Joy," "Fare Thee Well Old Joe Clark,"
"Under the Double Eagle." I never knew
How anybody could hold a banjo
Any such a way and still be able
To play it, but she did. Many a time,
When I was a little girl, I could hear
Miss Ruby's banjo come tinkling across
The holler. Sometimes it'd make our old dog
Buddy commence to howling. My daddy'd come
Out on the porch and holler "Whoa here Buddy!

Shut that ruckus up! You hear me?" And then
The banjo playing would stop, and my daddy
He'd shout across the holler "Never you mind
This old hound, Miss Ruby! He ain't got no sense.
Play 'Shady Grove' for me." And she would.

Anyway, that was long before they built
The dam, before Miss Ruby got the skin cancer.
I recollect it was nineteen and forty-six
When they started the dam. I guess Miss Ruby
Must've been getting on toward seventy then.
She got the cancer a year or two before
They moved her off her place. That woman suffered,
Especially during the summer, what with
The heat and the flies and all. Her daughter,
Lavelle, took good care of her, though, until
The very end. Lord knows it must not
Have been easy. I don't know if I
Could've done what she did.

                                        When the Corps
Of Engineers first started coming around,
Telling folks about how they were going
To build the dam, some people were all for it,
For the electricity and all, and some
Were against it. Just like it is with the
New North/South highway, I guess. Then as now,
It seems like it was mostly the younger ones
That were for it. And so many of them
Ended up moving away, anyway.

The older folks though had lived on their farms
All their lives, and their people before them.
Some of them got plain riled at these TVA men
For telling them they had to move off
The old home place because they were going
To flood it. Bury a perfectly good
Farm under water. It just didn't make sense.
But it was plain as day they were going
To do it. It was just a matter of when.
They got senators and congressmen and such
To come and speak about it. Finally,
Most realized it wouldn't do any good
To try and hold out and just took the money
And moved further up on the ridges. It was
The saddest thing to see some of those families
Leave their farms. They'd pack everything they owned
Up in the wagon and then just stand out there
On the road. And then after a long time
They'd finally call to the mules and the wagon
Would start creeping up the ridge so slow
You'd have thought the water would get there
Before they got away. Seems I recall
Ardy Bransom took his porch apart
And took it with him.

        Miss Ruby, though, she
Was a fighter. She wouldn't leave for no
Amount of money. The chairman of the whole
TVA—Morgan was his name—even came
Down from Washington, D.C. and sat on

Miss Ruby's porch and tried to get her to
Take the money and leave. They offered her
More money, but she wouldn't go. "I was born
In this house, and I aim to die in this house,"
She would tell them. Then they offered to move
The house. She wouldn't hear of it. Finally—
And this is the part I like the best—
They had to send in a Federal Marshall
With an eviction notice and a bunch
Of corpsmen to escort her off her property.
Miss Ruby just sat in her rocker
With her banjo in her lap and wouldn't budge.
The corpsmen finally picked her up, rocker and all,
And carried her to their truck.

                              I was sitting
In our kitchen, across the holler, while all
This was going on. All of a sudden
I heard Miss Ruby's banjo, and then
A bunch of voices I didn't recognize.
I ran out the back door and up to the top
Of the hill behind the tobacco patch
Where you could look across and down to
The Donaldson place. There was Miss Ruby,
Sitting just as stiff as always in her
Rocker in the bed of the truck, just playing
The living daylights out of her banjo.
I remember it was "Shady Grove" she played.
I never heard her play it so fast or so loud.

Moonrise at Dale Hollow Lake

Later,
as evening's dark hand
stills the water

and tourists glide
like boats to their homes,
I sit with friends

on an island point
and watch the moon
dance above cedars,

its reflection
fanning out
across black water.

A fish rises
as though to strike
the feathered light.

Something just this side
of saying
aches in my jaw.

House Burning

This is the story of my grandparents' house
Burning. I'll set it out as straight as I can.
Some things I've forgot and some, I own,
I never knew, but what I do recall has ran

Through my head for nearly twenty years, and this,
Though a little spruced up, is that. I am ten
Years old—Summer, 1964—and light
In sheets and waves rises from the chicken

Coop's tin roof. Out back of the house, high up
In the limbs of an old cherry tree, I sit
Lighting firecrackers (Black Cat) to scare away
Blackbirds. It's misting rain, and the smell of chicken shit,

Wet tree bark and wild mint mingle in the air—
That smell being one of the things I can't
Get out of my head. Anyhow, I've been
Here visiting for a week, and right now the slant

Of light through the trees tells me it's almost lunch,
Besides which I smell chicken frying, and it
Being Sunday I expect my folks will come
Driving in soon from Hunter's Point to visit,

And later take me home, though I'm not
Much inclined to go. Am more inclined
To stay and, later this evening, go fishing
With Papa, though I always get snagged and wind

In nothing, not even hook and sinker. But now
MeeMa's calling from the back kitchen window:
"Child, come down from there; you'll fall and break your neck!
They'll be here directly. Now you go

And get washed up and come on in to eat."
They came—Mom, Dad, sister, little brother—
And we ate until about to bust. Then
Dad drove down to visit my other grandmother.

Pretty soon Papa left to go to town
To the Sunday drawing. I wanted to go
Too—to see the old men whittling and chewing
Tobacco, and who won what—but Mama said no,

You've got to stay and be the man of the house.
So we were all drowsing in the front bedroom,
Counting seconds between lightning and thunder—
My brother nibbling in the kitchen—when *BOOM!*

The house shuddered, sparks flew, and my brother
In the kitchen doorway, framed in crackling
Silent-movie light, screamed bloody murder.
"Man of the house"—the thought went rattling

Through my head. My brother ran to the bedroom
Where we all stood, our eyes frozen to the ceiling,
The overload spitting through the wiring—
Jagged black snakes, plaster dust, paint peeling.

"It must've struck the fuse box!" MeeMa yelled.
Mama was on the phone: "Get me the fire
Department—lightning's struck Jewell Terry's place!"
But they couldn't come that far, and then the wire

Sparked and the phone went dead. "Bob, you and Brett
Run over and tell Rink what's happened and stay
There." Rink Pruett rented from my grandparents.
We ran, barefoot, down the gravel driveway

And up the road to his house. "Rink! Rink!" we
Burst in. "MeeMa's house is on fire. It's burning!"
He and his wife Mattie Mae were shelling
Peas, which flew everywhere, the pan turning

Over as he jumped up. Nobody made
Us stay, so we didn't. By now the smoke
Rolled thick and black out of all the windows,
And even though it seemed the rain should soak

Everything and slow it down, it didn't seem
To help. My sister ran around to ring
The dinner bell, hoping neighbors would hear,
And I went inside. You couldn't see a thing

For all the smoke. Choking, I found a window
And poked my head out for air. There was my
Sister in the side yard, downed power lines
Jumping and spitting all around her. I

Tried to scream, but couldn't. Just then I heard
My mother's voice, over by the stairwell.
"You can't! You can't!" she hollered, and I crawled
Over there, just as MeeMa slapped holy hell

Out of my mother. "Let me go, damn it!
I can't lose everything!" But my mom she
Dragged her down the stairs and over to Rink
Who shook her and held her and called to me

To goddam get the hell out, which I did.
A crowd of neighbors had gathered and were
Carrying out what they could. I had
Forgotten about my sister but saw her

And my brother out front, both O.K. Then
Something fell—*Clunk*—at my feet. A snuff tin.
"What the . . ." Then another one, and a third.
People were looking up. There, with a grin,

At the upstairs window was Paul Johnson,
Who, most said, was "a little tetched." He threw
Down another tin (he collected them),
And then some empty pop bottles. Paul knew

What was important to him and figured
It was the same with everybody. "Paul!"
Yelled Andrew Johnson. "The house is going.
You'll have to jump! This mattress'll break your fall."

Fearless and erect, like any good soldier,
Paul saluted and, right hand over heart,
Jumped. He hit the mattress and was out cold.
He came to a minute later with a start

As my grandfather's gas tank, by the tractor shed,
Went fireballing skyward. "Praise God, I've done
Died and gone to hell!" he wailed, pitifully,
And passed out again. By this time someone

Had gotten word down to Papa and Dad.
We were all standing around out front when,
Creaking and groaning, the thing finally caved in—
Just shuddered down into coals. One old hen

That had been cautiously eyeing the show
Jumped and squawked away. What else can I tell?
There wasn't much saved; it happened too fast.
Nobody knows how Paul got up there. Hell

Couldn't keep him; he got all right. That night
My MeeMa and Papa went home with us.
I don't know about anybody else.
I was changed. I'd never heard MeeMa cuss.

I felt good. I felt I'd done some growing up.
"Trial by fire," I repeated again and again.
That night, in my bed, I went to sleep and dreamed
Not of fire, but of standing among men.

Reeling In

In the days of his dying, my grandfather Terry
would sit afternoons by his new pond fishing,
his body motionless except
for the good right arm, casting
again and again the red-and-white bobber
out to the pond's center,
then reeling it in
through the wash of each slowly spreading
concentric wave.

Later, in the cool of evening,
the air damp and thrilling
with thunder, he'd sit
on the porch in a gaunt iron chair,
three coats of paint flaking,
and tell me again the old story—
how he, only twenty, having just married
my grandmother the schoolteacher
and anxious to prove himself
farming her people's land,
would be out before sun-up,
two fifty-pound bags of seed corn
strapped to his back, sowing
the Knob on a contour.
He'd do it for days, all day walking
the newly plowed ground,
then do it all over again, shouldering
fertilizer instead of seed.

He told me less about when he ran
with a mean bunch of brothers,
the Stones, from Turkey Creek.
"Shotgun," they called him,
his middle name being Winchester.
"Sometimes I feel like I've lived
two or three lives," he'd say.

And when he'd fall asleep
in the chair in the fragrant dusk,
head thrown back, fingers
laced over his belly, taking his ease
after eighty years, two or three lives,
I'd close my eyes and see my grandfather,
"Shotgun" Terry, six-foot-four, the sun
exploding from his blond hair,
come striding through concentric waves of corn,
not an ounce of anything on his back.

The Reverend Moody Montgomery Takes Up Serpents for the First and Last Time

Like his Bible of Hell, which Blake said
His readers would have "whether they will
Or no," this orphan tale, this infernal
Yarn, is yours, Hunter's Point. The truth
Will out—I was there. It's all well and good
To claim as your own that fine, that great man,
Cordell Hull—"Tennessee's Soldier-Statesman"
Boasts the tarnished plaque on the courthouse
Square. But where is Moody's Memorial?
"Tennessee's Shyster-Snake Handler"—How's that?
"Oh, no. No. That happened up in Kentucky.
Harlan, I believe." Twenty years since
And still the story's traded, like a load
Of unclaimed moonshine, between Hunter's Point
And Harlan. Peace, Moody Montgomery—
Your unquiet shade here will have its rest.
Accept, Hunter's Point, your prodigal. The truth
Will out—I was there.

                    Hunter's Point Church of Christ,
No, let me get my theology right—
"The Church of Christ Meeting at Hunter's Point"—
The point being that the church *house* is one
Thing, and of little moment, and *The Church*—
That is, the members—is the very body
Of Christ, and like as not the only thing

Keeping this sinful world fast from the fires
Of a vengeful and jealous God. And fine
Distinctions being part and parcel
Of the Church of Christ's history, you can
File this one alongside such momentous
involvements as "Is It a Sin for a
Woman to Cut Her Hair?" "The Evils
Of the Modern Dance." "The Heresy
Of Instrumental Music." And this last,
Particularly subtle, "Should a Christian
Drink Coca-Cola?" Alas, I have no
Easy answers. Can only say, along
With St. Paul, "This is a Great Mystery."
Or quote Faulkner's marvelous boy, Quentin,
Called to witness, "You would have to be born there."

It was in August of Nineteen Sixty-Five,
A locust summer, and dry as any
I can remember, that Grady McKamey
And I were down by the cattle pond playing
With the wooden wind-up paddle boats
My grandfather had made us. "Gimme yours,"
Grady said. "My rubber band broke." Grady
Was sixteen, three years older than me,
And big for his age. Once, a couple of years
Before, we were wrestling in the corncrib
And he sat on me so that it hurt
To breathe for three days. I gave it to him.
"Betcha didn't know my Uncle Moody's
Comin' in tomorrow," he said, winding

The boat's sliver of a paddle. "Did too.
Besides which, he's not your uncle. He's some
Kind of cousin-thrice-removed or something."
I'd heard my grandmother the night before
Talking on the phone to Lula Mae Reno,
Who ran the store at Hunter's Point, about
Moody Montgomery. "Can't mean no good,"
She had said. "I hate to think what
T. Thompson'll do if he starts foolin'
Around with that little Velma again."
"The only place he *removed* to is
Apalachacola," Grady sniffed. "He just
Got an Associated Degree in
Psychological Counseling at
Buncombe Bible College. Besides, he's a lot
More fun than any old uncle, anyway.
Last time he's home me and him went up
To the Milford graveyard one night and got
Drunker'n Cootie Brown on some 'shine he got
Down at old man Stone's." The rubber band
He'd been winding broke with a snap and wound
Itself around his finger. "Dogshit!" he said.
"I'm goin' home."

                The reason for Moody's return,
My grandmother told me that night over
Popcorn and 7-Up, was that since he
Now had a degree from Bible College,
He was going to conduct a Gospel
Tent Meeting at Hunter's Point Church of Christ

Because Brother Lambert had to go to Detroit
To preach his father's funeral. My grandfather,
Who until this time had been absorbed
In *The Wilburn Brothers Show* on T.V.,
Half-strangled on his 7-Up and snorted,
"Mark my words, no good'll come of that!"
Since he was an Elder of the church,
And not a man to mince words, I pondered
What he'd said, and wondered why they'd decided
To let Moody preach the meeting in the first place.
My grandmother wiped her hands and went back
To her crocheting.

               "Moody's got a plan
And you and me's got to help him," Grady said,
Smearing a mosquito across his forehead.
It was Friday night, and the first I'd seen
Of Grady since Moody had come in
On Wednesday. I split open a paw-paw
With the new Barlow knife my grandfather
Had given me for helping him get in hay.
"I bet I know what kind of plan Moody's
Got in mind," I said. "My grandad'd love
That—me gettin' involved in some scheme
Of Moody Montgomery's. Uh-uh. No way."
"All's we gotta do is catch him three
Hog-nosed snakes," Grady continued, as though
I'd never opened my mouth. I gave him half
Of the paw-paw, which was juicy and smelled
Like an over-ripe banana. "Hog-nosed snakes?

What's he want 'em for?" "You know Velma Thompson?"
(Oh Lord, I thought) "Well, she's a little bit
Of a Holy Roller, see? Only there
Ain't no Holy Roller church around here—
Just the Church of Christ. Anyhow, Moody's
Got the hots for Velma Thompson, and
Sunday night, when the meetin' starts, he's gonna
Pretend like he's one of them snake-handlin'
Preachers—like what's down around Chattanooga.
Moody figures that'll have her eatin'
Out of his hand." "Wait a minute," I said.
"For one thing, Velma Thompson's married—
To T. Thompson, who's big and ugly and mean.
For another thing, there's no *way* they're gonna
Allow no snake handling in the church, and
For *another* thing, them Chattanooga
Snake handlers handle *rattlesnakes*, not little
Ol' hog-nosed snakes. Moody's got shit for brains."
"Them what's got shit for brains do not get
Degrees in Psychological Counseling,"
Grady said indignantly. "Moody's thought
It all out: T. Thompson's in Florida
Runnin' produce. Won't be back till next
Wednesday. Second, he's got this crate that says
AUDIO-VISUAL AIDS—he's gonna put
The snakes in that and tell 'em he's gonna
Illustrate his preachin', like they taught him
At Buncombe. And third, he wants hog-nosed snakes
'Cause they *look* like rattlesnakes but don't bite.
Are you in?" "No, I am not," I said,

Cleaning the knife blade on my pants leg.
"Pansy. I thought you'd do it just for fun.
I guess that means Moody won't be takin'
Us to Harlan to the dance hall in his
GTO next Friday night." Suddenly,
Moody's crazy scheme began to seem
A good bit more plausible, especially since
Before this whole business about Moody
Had come up, Grady and I had been
Sitting under the paw-paw tree, lusting
For The Evils of the Modern Dance. Still,
I had doubts. "Well, I'm still not too sure . . ."
"Do you want me to set on you again?"
That clinched it. "I'm in," I said.

                              Grady caught
Two snakes; I had to catch the other one.
Saturday afternoon I was poking
Around some groundhog holes with a snake stick
In the woods between my grandfather's place
And Thompson's. I was pretty sure I'd find
One there, and was bent over investigating
A potential snake hole when suddenly
Everything went dark. I craned my head around
And felt myself dwindle away to nothing
In the gigantic shadow of T. Thompson.
"M-Mr. Thompson!" I stammered. "Moody said
You wouldn't be back till Wednesday!" "Moody!"
He spat through the gap where his front teeth
Used to be. "Moody Montgomery?

That bastard is *why* I'm back. I heard
He'd come slinkin' back here—the weasel!
How come him to be knowin' so much
About my business? And how come you
To be knowin' he knows? You know somethin'
Boy, and I aim to find it out. What the hell
You doin' with that snake stick?" All the while
He'd been talking my mind had been stuck
On a scene from the past summer. I'd come
Into town with my grandfather who'd gone
Into the hardware store. As I sat
On a bench outside the courthouse, T. Thompson
And a man I didn't know came around
The corner. "What does the 'T' stand for?"
The man said. "Stand for?" said T. Thompson.
"It stands for *me*. What does a body's name
Usually stand for?" "Stands for me!" the man
Repeated in a loud voice. He slapped his knee
And laughed. "Whoo! That's a good 'un!" T. Thompson
Though apparently didn't think it was
"A good 'un." He spat something brown and sticky
Onto the man's shoe. When the man looked down,
He brought his fist down hard on the man's neck,
And when the man sort of crumpled he brought
His knee up hard into the man's face. The man
Fell in a heap on the street in the Sheriff's
Parking space. T. Thompson stalked off. Across
The street, in Milford's Drug Store, I could see
The Sheriff, drinking a coke, watching.
"Me and Mr. Terry's been good neighbors

For a good long while—I'd shore as hell hate
To see anything happen to his grandson."
The voice of the real T. Thompson snapped
Me back to reality. "Now talk," he said,
Backing me against a tree. "About
Moody Montgomery." I spilled my guts.
I told him why Moody had come back,
I told him about the Tent Meeting, about
Velma, about me and Grady and the snakes,
I told him about Harlan, the dance hall,
The GTO, I think I mentioned
Something about paw-paws. I babbled. I *sang*.
"That's enough," T. Thompson said. "I git the picture."
I was still against the tree. He leaned
Even closer. I felt dizzy. I felt
Like I was going to fall into that
Black space where his teeth used to be. "All I want
Is to know where you're goin' to keep them snakes.
That's all I want to know." "In a crate
In my grandma's henhouse," I said. "Good boy.
See? That's all I wanted to know." Then his
Face clouded again. "Tell anybody
You seen me and you'll regret it." Then he smiled,
And then laughed. "A snake in the henhouse—
That's a good 'un!" he said, and turned and walked
Away. I sank down onto a gnarled root
And shook.

Sunday morning I pretended sick.
My grandmother was dubious, but let

Me stay home from church anyway. "You don't
Look too awful peaked," she said. "Less you're
Dyin', you'll have to go tonight. It's the first
Night of the Meetin'." I watched from my
Upstairs window as the red-and-white
Bel-Air lumbered down the rutted driveway,
Leaving a cloud of yellow dust hanging
In the air behind it. "Thank you, God,"
I said aloud, "for helping me not to murder
Grady McKamey at church this morning."
I hadn't slept at all Saturday night.
T. Thompson had scared the bejesus
Out of me. When I couldn't keep myself
From thinking about it I started
Shaking again. Every now and then I'd
Go to the back window and stare out
At the henhouse. I knew something awful was up,
But I couldn't imagine what. A little
After twelve my grandparents came home.
I ate some crackers and drank a coke while
They had Sunday dinner. "Grady was asking
About you at church this morning," my
Grandmother began. "He said he'd come by
This afternoon and check up on you."
"Oh," I said. "I believe I'll go back upstairs."

"Well, did you get it?" Grady said, eating
A piece of fried chicken my grandmother
Had given him. "Get what?" "The *snake*, you fool."
"Oh. Oh yeah. I got it. They're in the henhouse."

"Good. I can't wait. What's wrong with you, anyhow?
How come you wasn't at church this morning?
You better be there tonight." "I just didn't
Want to go to church twice in one day, O.K.?
I'll be there." "O.K. Me and Moody'll
Sneak around back this evenin' and get the snakes.
See you tonight." "Yeah, right." I'd never before
Felt snakes were any more evil than any
Other creature, but now I was beginning
To wonder.

                    The tent was one of those big
Brown rectangular ones Hassell and Greef's
Funeral Home usually set up when someone
Important died, or the Optimist Club,
Of which Mr. Hassell was president,
Needed it to fry fish in at the
County Fair. Grady and I sat in wooden
Folding chairs, about five rows back, behind
The Elders and Deacons. Sterling Simpson,
The song leader, had just announced number
45. He struck his tuning fork
On his shoe, held it to his ear, and began,
Giving the congregation their notes—
Fa - Sa - Me - Do, nasal tenor slicing thick air:

> *This world is not my home*
> *I'm just a-passin' through*
> *My treasures are laid up*
> *Somewhere beyond the blue*

The Angels beckon me
Down from Heaven's open door
And I can't feel at home
In this world any more

After a few more songs, Moody Montgomery
Came striding in from somewhere outside.
He looked sharp in his blue double-breasted
Suit, and had on one of the biggest,
Reddest ties I had ever seen. I glanced
Uneasily over at the dull wooden
Crate with AUDIO-VISUAL AIDS
Stencilled on it in red. I felt Grady's
Elbow touch my ribs. I couldn't concentrate
And needed to use the bathroom. "BROTHERS
AND SISTERS," Moody fairly shouted, "I WANT
TO TALK TO YOU TONIGHT ABOUT FAITH. FAITH
AS A GRAIN OF MUSTARD SEED—PRAISE THE LORD—
FAITH TO MOVE MOUNTAINS. I WANT TO TALK TO YOU
ABOUT THE POWER OF *JESUS*, ah, MOVING
IN YOU, MOVING IN ME, ah. TURN, IF YOU WILL,
IN YOUR BIBLES TO MARK XVI, VERSES
17 AND 18, WHERE THE LORD *JESUS*, ah,
SAYS: AND THESE SIGNS SHALL FOLLOW THEM THAT
    BELIEVE, ah—
THAT'S YOU AND *ME*, BROTHERS AND SISTERS—
IN MY NAME SHALL THEY CAST OUT DEVILS, ah,
THEY SHALL SPEAK WITH NEW TONGUES—
    PRAISE THE LORD!—
THEY SHALL TAKE UP SERPENTS—OLD SATAN

HIMSELF, BROTHERS AND SISTERS, THEY SHALL TAKE
HIM UP!" I heard a few scattered Amen's,
One or two Praise the Lord's! "AND IF THEY DRINK, ah,
ANY DEADLY THING, IT SHALL NOT HURT THEM . . ."
Moody was gesturing with the Bible, throwing
His arms wide in the air, sweating, brushing
The oily loop of hair repeatedly
From his forehead. A second later
And he had a snake in one hand—rigid,
Sinuous, awful—its pale yellow
Underbelly and brown speckled diamonds
Alternately flashing in the harsh light
Of the naked bulbs. A murmur had begun
From nowhere in particular or
Everywhere at once. Chairs scraped. Men's voices
Thrummed. "I AM NOT, BROTHERS AND SISTERS,
A MIRACLE WORKER, ah, I AM A MAN
OF *FAITH*!" My grandfather started toward him.
Suddenly, there was a loud crash—I looked
Back and saw Velma Thompson writhing
On the ground, moaning. Then from somewhere
Nearby, I heard a dry, insistent rhythm,
Like the locusts, only higher, louder.
I cut my eyes toward Grady. He was
Looking back at Velma, but in his hand,
Near his thigh, was a little pink-and-blue
Baby rattle. I reached for his hand and knocked
It out into the aisle. People stared.
For a second, everything got real quiet—
I looked at Moody, holding the snake.

Moody stared at the snake. The snake opened
Its mouth, tracing a graceful figure 8.
Then the dry, insistent rhythm began
Again. I glared at Grady. "Sweet Jesus
On a Stick! That's a timber rattler
He's got!" Grady hollered. The rattler struck
And Moody sank to his knees, the snake
Hanging limp from his neck. In the awful
Silence that followed, a great hulking figure
Came striding forward. It was T. Thompson.
"I reckon I got some confessin' to do,"
He said, and the tent seemed to explode
With screaming women, shouting men, crying
Babies, and seemed to fly straight up, spinning,
Spinning, far into the blackness of night.

Working for Roger

——for Bill Thompson and Kristi Umbreit

We came to Memphis in the godawful
Summer of 1980. Which is when,
If you recall, everything went to hell—
The economy, anyway. I'd been

Working on my Masters at UNC,
Married a year, when my wife got word
She'd been accepted to Med School in Memphis—
I finished up, and off we went. I'd heard

Some less than charitable things about Memphis—
About Med School, too, for that matter.
I remembered the newscasts after
Dr. King was shot—seeing people scatter

As the tanks went clanking through the center
Of town. "Med students are completely mad,"
A friend had said. "Good luck." There'll be hard times,
I thought, but surely it won't be that bad.

I was wrong. The trip to Memphis was killing—
104 degrees, the U-Haul
Stuffed, axles bowing. Just east of Memphis
I-40 peters out and you crawl

Through parts of town you never visit again.
We stopped in front of Ruby's Disco Diner
To call for directions. I heard Mary scream.
A Cadillac Seville that had seen finer

Days went hurtling through Ruby's plate-glass window.
I jumped in the truck as a middle-aged
Man emerged, stumbling and cursing the rubble.
I backed the truck out as he stood there and raged—

We got where we were going on our own.
I fancy myself a writer, and I think
In terms of symbols and foreshadowing—
I'll say no more. We set up house in the stink

And roar of downtown Memphis. There was no work
For a callow English major, just out
Of college. I did odd jobs—custodial,
Construction—and we starved until about

Mid-October when I got a part-time
Teaching slot, evenings, at a local college:
Two nights a week, twenty students, mostly
Adult—so eager to learn it took the edge

Off my inexperience. I taught the course
Once through and did a decent job—got hired
To do it again in the spring. And that's
Where I met Roger. He sat up front, wired

To a tape recorder, which bothered me
A little. He always seemed tired, or tense,
Or maybe both. He was just past forty,
Short and paunchy, and quick to take offense.

Oh, he was politeness itself to me, but
His gray eyes and square jaw reminded me
Of a high school bully I'd known. He wrote
Pretty well—had, at mid-quarter, a solid "B."

Still, he always worried about his grade;
Would call, usually in the middle
Of one of mine and Mary's arguments—
Things weren't going too well with us, little

Things would set us off—and hem and haw,
Wondering wasn't there something he could do
To make sure he did well. Near the quarter's end
We talked politics in class one night: who

The present economy hurt, and who
It helped. At end of class I jokingly said
"Does anybody want to hire a poor
English teacher, full-time?" Roger cocked his head,

Gave me a funny look. He hung around
Till everyone had gone, then asked me
"Did you really mean it, what you said up there?
About needin' work? If you did then we

Might could work somethin' out. I'm a contractor,
See. Not workin' much now, though, on account
Of I'm bein' audited by the Feds—
That bid-riggin' stuff. What I did don't amount

To much, but I gotta lay low for awhile.
Anyhow, I got this cabin on a lake
Down in Mississippi I'm workin' on—
Cuttin' grass, plumbing, stuff like that—you'd make

Five bucks an hour. What d'ya say?" We needed
Money; I said O.K. "All right. Meet me
Saturday at, uh—you know Kitty's Place?"
I did. It was in the news constantly.

One of Danny Dixon's topless clubs.
If Kitty's went a month without a bust
That was news. "Yeah, I know it," I said.
"Meet me there at nine o'clock. And just

Keep this to yourself, O.K.?" I figured
He didn't want anyone at the school
To think he was bribing me for a grade.
Just the same, I felt uneasy. The fool

Things I do for money, I sighed. Saturday
Dawned hot and muggy. Roger was sitting
In his truck—a blue, metal-flake monster—
Talking to someone, occasionally spitting

Out the window. It was Danny Dixon.
I recognized him from the news. "Well, well,
Here comes the professor himself. Jack Lynch,
Meet Danny Dixon. We used to raise hell

Together, back in high school. I built this place
For Danny—even did a decent job,
If I say so myself." "Nice t'meetcha,"
Dixon drawled. "Same to you." "Well, I'd hob-nob

With you all day Rog, but I got work to do.
Be seein' ya." And so we took off, down
I-55 toward Mississippi.
Roger was chewing a toothpick. A frown

Shifted it to one side. "Me and Danny
Was talkin' about this whore—well, she's
One of his dancers, Candy's her name—
Tall, good figure, pretty as you please,

But a whore just the same. Well anyhow,
This old girl went out on a call last week—
Turned out to be a *judge*. And what d'ya guess
He wanted her to do, huh? Take a leak—

On him. Never in my life heard such shit.
Now just what do you make of that, Jack?" How
Do I get myself into these things, I wondered.
"That's really not my business, is it now,

Roger? How he gets off I mean. How far
Is it to your cabin?" "About ten miles
South of Hernando—Lake Cinderella."
"I figured Arkabutla." "Nothin' riles

Me more'n them city folks in their power boats—
Cinderella's outta the way. I got
Ten acres to myself. Look—there's The Killer's
House—Jerry Lee. My uncle sold him that spot.

Y'know, some people say he's for real
A killer. Got any idea how many
Wives he's gone through? I forget. It's a sight, though.
He's been charged with all kinds of things. Not any

Ever stick. He's Hernando's favorite son.
Got his own club—Hernando's Hideaway.
We oughta go there sometime—take the wives.
Have a little fun afterwards. What say?"

"Uh, yeah . . . Maybe." I didn't like the way
He'd said "fun." "How far now?" "Just down this hill."
Below us, the whole delta lay steaming.
To the right was a swamp; left, a landfill.

Roger swung the truck to the left, just past
The dump, and up a steep grade. "This is it."
It was green, shingled, set back into the hill.
Down and to the left was a scummy bit

Of backwater. Not fancy, but peaceful,
Like he'd said. "Get the tools. I'll open her up."
I grabbed the sling and went to work on the weeds.
He stayed inside, drinking whiskey from a cup.

I don't mind snakes, just as long as they don't
Surprise me—this one did. About three feet
Long, red and brown. "A cottonmouth!" I thought—
But not on land. "Come in outta the heat!

Dinner time!" Roger yelled. The snake looped off.
"We got vieenies and crackers," he said,
"And water if you want it." The radio
Played country music. Tammy Wynette led

Into a station break: "Ladies and gents,"
A nasal voice whined, "This is Buddy Bond,
Invitin' you to hear me and my band,
The Bondsmen, at Bond's Barn . . ." "Well I'm not fond

Of Buddy Bond," Roger croaked. "Sawed-off runt—
Always wanted to be big as Jerry Lee.
He ain't even close—only in his head.
Besides, he likes the little boys, y'see.

Got in trouble for it a coupla years back.
Folks don't mind him though—runs a topless joint
And porno house on highway 65,
Plays there with his band. I'll make it a point

To pay you for all day if you'll take off
Fishin' with me." It was hot, and the snake
Had spooked me. "It's a deal," I said. We put out
In a battered green canoe, its tiny wake

Webbing the viscous backwater. "You know
Why I'm takin' that class?" he said. "It's 'cause
One of these days I'm gonna write my memoirs.
For my son, for Little Roger. I've broke laws,

Bootlegged, messed around and even killed a man
Twenty years ago—didn't mean to. Fought
All my life. You have to when you start out
At rock bottom. I don't want Roger caught

Like I been caught all my life. I send him
To a private school, try to act right
In front of him. Even go to church, though
My heart's not in it. He won't have to fight

Just to grow up; just to get a piece
Of some little somethin'; just to get *by*.
And then, one day when he's old enough,
I'll take it out and say 'This is no lie.

This is the story of your old man's life.
Thank him and God you've got it better. Make
Somethin' of yourself.' And if he's ashamed
Of what I've done, I'll come down to this lake

And won't nobody hear from me again."
The setting sun fired the water bronze,
Glittered on the fat bluegill we'd hauled in.
"They don't grow like that in Tennessee ponds,"

He laughed. "They're yours. Take 'em home to the wife.
We'd best be gettin' on back. Folks get wild
'Round here Saturday nights." He was quiet
All the way back. The night was windy, but mild.

He let me off, handing me two twenties.
"Later, Doc." Between the trunks of two old walnuts,
On a concrete slab I scaled and cleaned the catch.
Something was there to be read in those guts.

John Lee Hooker

Boom Boom Boom Boom! John Lee Hooker's in town,
And Memphis holds its breath as the Kingsnake stomps
To splinters the rickety stage. The swamps
Beyond the bridge tremble. New Madrid slides down.
His voice, a raw, raucous rumble we drown
In, swoops, slides, simmers, soothes, and Hooker chomps
His pipestem, leans into the story and whomps
His Gibson a lick or two in G. A frown
Creases the cracked leather of his fine face
And his dark glasses fog. Ancient as the river
Two blocks over, he conjures devil weather—
The great flood of Tupelo—and to that place,
And us, listening, declares "I won't ever
Forget it, and I know you won't either."

LEARNING HOW TO LIVE

Loveless You Wander

Places chip away at you,
the only
figure in the landscape.

You travel through lives
easy as a salesman
through towns, states.

Chameleonlike you offer
the perfect pitch:

In Boise they loved
the Horatio Alger number—
"Scarcely modified," you said.

In Bayonne, it was
early Brando, updated.

And how they roared, the good
citizens of Duluth,
at your tales
of the pathetic rubes in Boise:
The undertaker
who could recite "Thanatopsis"
but always broke down in tears
at all those who *shall leave*

their mirth and their employments,
and shall come
and make their bed with thee.

Loveless you wander
the riotous world,
God's plenty
strewn in your wake,
the road you will take
straight and clear before you
as far as it goes.

In Thrall

Terra Incognita:
The logic of night
upon me. By my own hand,
with warp of muscle
and woof of nerve
on a loom of bone,
the black flag
of despair wove.
And so drifted,
snapped loose
from soil and sense:
shadow on the land,
shiver along the spine.
Distinction fled.
Boundaries wavered,
Dissolved: the world
a mire of nacre.
Terra Incognita:
The logic of night
upon me.

Winding Down

Sometimes it seems like bedtime, but it's not, really. At the corners of your closed eyes are whole swarms of light, artlessly gossiping of objects they have struck, anxious to know if there's anything left worth reporting to. And all this is going on it seems somewhere very far from you, as though you were buried under snow. And it keeps on not quite being like that until finally the gentle clamor overcomes you. "It's all over," you think. You open your eyes and in comes all that light, chattering like excited children, filled with news of the room! How the boots still stand in the corner where you took them off, although now one bows at the break, like a shy animal nuzzling. How the fiddle, propped against the chair, shifted a fraction of an inch the last time the furnace clicked on. How in fact the whole room has subtly altered since the last time you arranged it in your mind. So you lie there, awash in the warm shiver of a yawn and stretch, cataloging this latest report of the room's half-life, the honey of light filling up your cells. Soon you will sleep, but not yet.

After Rilke

I

In what tree was the rising
 fog making its nest? What voices
sang in the trees' weaving
of light to leaf?

Shhh!
So much talk, so many questions . . .
Don't you know silence
is the great doctor? The universal
antidote? If you can, just walk.
All around you, the forest shivers
in anticipation.
A wordless song of endless arrival
is the prize you win
for your patience, your longing,
your abandonment of storied artifice.
See! All around you your green home.

II

And so I walked,
my footsteps sifting through leaves,
and found a girl

asleep in the grass.
In her ears, the forest
had planted itself
so that while she slept
everything there could listen.

And she never woke up
it was so quiet.

Birds sang through the stillness.

Her sleep was everything.

III

So tell me then, traveler:
where is the one road
that will bind you
like a child tethered
by his mother's cord?
And how will you call the sound
of your walking on it?

Think of the sound your living makes:
shuttle of breath
in the warp of air—
Perhaps that is the sound.

IV

Lonely, uncertain,
I carried the map of my goings
tattooed on my back
like a turtle
where I couldn't see it.

Because I was lost
I cried
and my tears fell on the leaves,
each the sound
of a tiny heartbeat.

Then suddenly a new rhythm!
And I knew it was her, waking.

Last Summer When the Moon

Dog days—
the earth closes
like a fist, a withered
flower, sweating it out.

You are in the west,
so far away my dreams
thin to a haze
in the evening's long light,
and I am still in the south,
marking time.

But I remember a night
last summer when the moon
rose, glistening, from the lake
of our bodies
and every tree
in my father's ten-acre wood
stuttered in that light.

The Life You've Led

falls away, piece by piece,
like the yellow leaves of aspen,
like scales from the blind man's eyes.

When the aspen's leaves have all fallen
we say it is bare—
might better say *naked*.

When the scales fall
from the blind man's eyes
we say it is a miracle,
but he is clumsy and afraid.

It is October, and yellow leaves
are falling everywhere.

I see your stark symmetry,
concealing green buds.

You see my amazed eyes.

How It Was

The twin waterfalls we stood under
late on a day in late autumn—
that's how it was inside my heart
whenever you spoke, or looked at me.
The arteries and veins, quicksilver streams
just under the surface of my skin.

The air of autumn shivers hot and cold
in and out of sunshine and shadow,
and that's how it was that brilliant day
inside my lungs, underneath my skin,
whenever you spoke, or looked at me.

The autumn leaves, touched by the sun,
explode in fever and fire,
and every time you touched me
that's how it was—
the long kiss, a brush of your hand—
little explosions everywhere
beneath the surface of my skin.

Night Music

i

The sky turns on a cricket's rasp
A voice smokes in the old chimney
Night sings like a fossil

ii

I hear feet
clump clump
down the alleyway
as darkness
blooms across the town

Look—
it's old beggar Night
spending the shadows
he's hoarded all day

Lights

i

This is the body's land—
at home here
or nowhere.
Through deep-welled air
the magnet moon
orients the singing
skin's cardinal points.

ii

In cedar hung silence,
through camp smoke and wave lap,
shards of stunned brightness
speak
a language of light.

iii

As from a great distance
patterns are seen
to shiver
suddenly into focus,
so these lights
flashing at the body's perimeter
connect
and in the vibrating darkness
chart our every step.

Climbing

—for Steve Thorne

High, this air—
wind-scrubbed and cold.

At eye level, above a near ridge,
a hawk hangs motionless
planing a shifting thermal.

Up here, an intuitive calculus
admitting no mistakes:

Rock threads the eye
of the body's needle
and we are sewn
into the wind's perfect dance.

The Naked Man in Briars

wondered why he'd ever come this way.

From their sunwarmed perches
snakes chuckled,
his predicament their pleasure.

Dire, Dire, the crows called
nasally through needle-thin beaks.

Lazily, and with delight,
the snakes uncoiled.

On sharp, hard rocks
the crows whetted their beaks.

The briars held the naked man.

All of a sudden, he thought he heard
something. Inwardly he listened,
as the leaden bell of the sky
rang inside his skin.

Bleeding and bitten the naked man
rose with relief
to the rigors of this world's work.

Ballade: Les Enfants du Soleil

I am bound on my most outward voyage.
—Mark Shearon

The eye of noon in splintered sky bleeding
Steely light onto the river below,
Steam rising like heat waves off tin sheeting,
Current pulsing in the water's marrow—
We strip in the bright air and find the flow.
The dark birds sing of journeys just begun
As our eyes touch their far flight and follow:
In hard air two hawks wheel into the sun.

The hand of night, a burnt-out bush leading
The wasted sun into its bleak shadow,
Moves on the hollow wind-road receding
Into the unblinking eye of a crow.
In the humming air all things follow slow.
We gaze up at the sky for direction
As roots of strange stars pierce our eyes and grow:
In dawn's air two hawks wheel into the sun.

The heart of morning, silver-pink, beating
In the eastern sky like an embryo,
Bursts open night's eerie womb repeating
Itself until our bodies come to glow.
On our eyes windy night begins to blow.

We rise up from our darkling dreams and run
To the river; our starry eyes burn low:
In bright air two hawks wheel into the sun.

The voice of this place is the wind's echo
Blessing the wild stars on which we reckon.
Dark wings in the sky plow a bright furrow:
In this air two hawks wheel into the sun.

Learning How to Live

I'm a starving man
in a large woolen coat
in summertime.

I'm not cold,
I'm hungry.

But the coat is all
I have and so
I wear the coat.

Notes

Letter to Ciardi: April 3, 1986
John Ciardi died on March 30, 1986. He was to have participated in a Literary Symposium on Saturday, March 29, at the University of Denver.

Fortune's Favorite Child
Based on the life and art of Walter Inglis Anderson, Mississippi painter and naturalist (1903-1965).

A Short History of Place
All are middle Tennessee place names.

Grateful thanks is given to the editors of the following journals, in which these poems have appeared, sometimes in slightly different form:

Asheville Poetry Review: "Three Voices from Hunter's Point"
Blue Plate Special: "En Passant: At Dinner"
Caesura: "After Rilke" and "Hearing Creeley Read"
Denver Quarterly: "Letter to Ciardi: April 3, 1986"
Georgia Journal: "The Naked Man in Briars"
The Georgia Review: "Loveless You Wander"
Lonzie's Fried Chicken: "Aging Gracefully" and "Learning How to Live"
Nebo: "House Burning" and "Miss Ida Belle McHenry Talks to the Man from the State 'Stories from Our Seniors' Project"
Negative Capability: "Once More, the Night" and "No Love Lost"
Now and Then: "Reeling In"
Pembroke Magazine: "Sunday Dinner"
Pikeville Review: "The Reverend Moody Montgomery Takes Up Serpents for the First and Last Time"
Poem: "Last Summer When the Moon," "The Life You've Led," "Ballade: Les Enfants du Soleil," and "Lights"
Prairie Schooner: "Handiwork" and "You"
The Small Farm: "Night Music (i)"
Southern Poetry Review: "Moonrise at Dale Hollow Lake"
The Vanderbilt Review: "How It Was" and "Winding Down"
Wood Ibis: "Climbing"

And the following anthologies:

"Winding Down": *Quantum Tao,* ed. Bradley Earle Hoge (Blue Heron Press, 1996)
"Handiwork": *Environment: Essence & Issue,* ed. Jim Villani (Pig Iron Press, 1992)
"Letter to Ciardi: April 3, 1986": *The Epistolary Form & The Letter as Artifact,* eds. Jim Villani and Naton Leslie (Pig Iron Press, 1992)

For their help, support, and encouragement, I would like to thank my family, my colleagues in the Department of English and Modern Languages at Barton College, the Writers Group of Wilson, Rough Mix and Friends, Ben Greene, Richard Parks, James Kibler, Bruce Bond, Bill Thompson, and Al Maginnes.

About the Author

Jim Clark was born in Byrdstown, Tennessee and educated at Vanderbilt University, the University of North Carolina at Greensboro, and the University of Denver. His poems and stories have appeared in *The Georgia Review, Prairie Schooner, Southern Poetry Review, Appalachian Heritage, Now & Then,* and in many other magazines and anthologies. He has been a scholar at the Bread Loaf Writers' Conference, and received the Harriette Simpson Arnow award. He has taught at Auburn University, directed the creative writing program at the University of Georgia, and is presently Writer-in-Residence at Barton College in Wilson, North Carolina. His first book of poems, *Dancing on Canaan's Ruins,* is now in its second printing.